FIVES SIXES AND SEVENS

FIVE

mpiled by Marjorie Stephenson with illustrations by Denis Wrigley

# IXES AND SEVENS

FREDERICK WARNE

Published by
FREDERICK WARNE & CO LTD: *London*
FREDERICK WARNE & CO LTD: *New York*

© *Frederick Warne & Co Ltd*
*London, England*
*1968*

*Reprinted 1970*

LIBRARY OF CONGRESS CATALOG CARD NO 69–11021

7232 0825 5
Printed by offset in Great Britain by
William Clowes & Sons Ltd, London and Beccles
1407.1169

# Contents

# Acknowledgements

The compiler and publishers wish to thank the following for their kind permission to reproduce poems:

**Fives**

Evans Brothers Ltd for "With a Hop and a Skip and a Jump" by W. O'Neill, "A Counting Rhyme" by M. M. Stephenson, "Following the Music" by Hilda I. Rostron and "You Do It Too" by Margaret Langford from *Child Education*, and "Ten Little Dicky-birds" by A. W. I. Baldwin from *A Book of a Thousand Poems*; Penguin Books Ltd for "Black Monkeys", "One, Two", "Acorn Bill", "The Snowman" and the riddles "I have Legs", "I have Teeth" and "I can Prick Your Finger" all by Ruth Ainsworth from *Lucky Dip* (Puffin Book); The Cresset Press for "Dogs" from *A Child's Dream* by Frances Cornford; A. & C. Black Ltd for "Clocks and Watches" from *Speech Rhymes*, edited by Clive Sansom; Miss Aileen Fisher for "After a Bath"; A. Wheaton & Co. Ltd and the author for "Runaway Engine" by Mollie Clarke from *Raggle Taggle Rhymes*; The estate of the late Miss Eleanor Farjeon for "Cats"; J. M. Dent & Sons Ltd and the Talbot Press for "Timothy Dan" by John D. Sheridan from *Stirabout Lane*.

"Kindness to Animals" is from *Tirra Lirra* by Laura E. Richards, by permission of Little, Brown and Co.

**Sixes**

Evans Brothers Ltd for "Zoo Manners" by Eileen Mathias, "November Glow" by Hilda I. Rostron and "Rufty and Tufty" by Isabell Hempseed from *A Book of a Thousand Poems*, and for "Tails" by Ivy Russell, "Autumn's Passing" by Hilda I. Rostron and "Red-currant Jelly" by M. M. Stephenson from *Child Education*; Dennis Dobson for "On the Ning Nang Nong" and "Down the Stream the Swans all Glide" from *Silly Verse for Kids* by Spike Milligan; A. & C. Black Ltd for "The Dustman" from *Speech Rhymes* edited by Clive Sansom; Miss Annie Cunningham for "I Caught a Fish" by Bertram Murray from *The Children's Choice*; The estate of the late Miss Eleanor Farjeon for "There are Big Waves" and "Cottage"; William Collins Sons and Co. Ltd for "Three Mice" by Charlotte Druitt Cole; A. B. Shiffrin for "Hide and Seek"; Oxford University Press for "Run a Little" from *The Blackbird in the Lilac* by James Reeves and "Grandad's Pipe" from *Happily Ever After* by Ian Serraillier; William Heinemann Ltd for "Waiting" from *The Wandering Moon* by James Reeves; Miss Mary Britton Miller for "The Cat"; The Literary Trustees of Walter de la Mare and The Society of Authors as their representative for "The Cupboard" by Walter de la Mare; Sidgwick & Jackson Ltd for "Choosing Shoes" by ffrida Wolfe from *The Very Thing*.

"Some Fishy Nonsense" is from *Tirra Lirra* by Laura E. Richards, by permission of Little, Brown and Co.

**Sevens**

William Heinemann Ltd for "The Elephant" from *Pillicock Hill* by Herbert Asquith, and "Animals' Houses" and "Rabbit and Lark" from *The Wandering Moon* by James Reeves; Oxford University Press for "Cows" from *Blackbird in the Lilac* by James Reeves; Mrs. Florence Page Jaques for "There Once Was a Puffin" from *Child Life* published by Rand McNally & Co.; National Christian Education Council for "Jack Frost" by Cecily E. Pike; J. M. Dent & Sons Ltd for "The Farmyard" from *Let's Enjoy Poetry*; Evans Brothers Ltd for "Red in Autumn" by Elizabeth Gould and "Caravans" by Irene Thompson, both from *A Book of a Thousand Poems*; Miss Emily Lewis for "My Dog"; The Literary Trustees of Walter de la Mare and The Society of Authors as their representative for "Some One" by Walter de la Mare; Dennis Dobson for "The Land of the Bumbley Boo" from *Silly Verse for Kids* by Spike Milligan; Sidgwick & Jackson Ltd for "The Boy with the Little Bare Toes" from *Gloucestershire Friends* by F. W. Harvey; The estate of the late Miss Eleanor Farjeon for "A Prayer for Little Things".

"Autumn Woods" from *A World to Know* by James S. Tippett is copyright 1933 by Harper & Brothers; renewed 1961 by Martha K. Tippett. "Familiar Friends" from *I Spend the Summer* by James S. Tippett is copyright 1930 by Harper & Brothers; renewed 1958 by James S. Tippett. "Chairoplane Chant" by Nancy Byrd Turner is from *Magpie Lane*, copyright 1927 by Harcourt, Brace & World, Inc.; renewed 1955 by Nancy Byrd Turner. Reprinted by permission of the publishers.

U.S.A. rights. "Run a Little" and "Cows" are from the book *The Blackbird in the Lilac* by James Reeves. Published 1959 by E. P. Dutton & Co., Inc. and reprinted with their permission.

# Fives

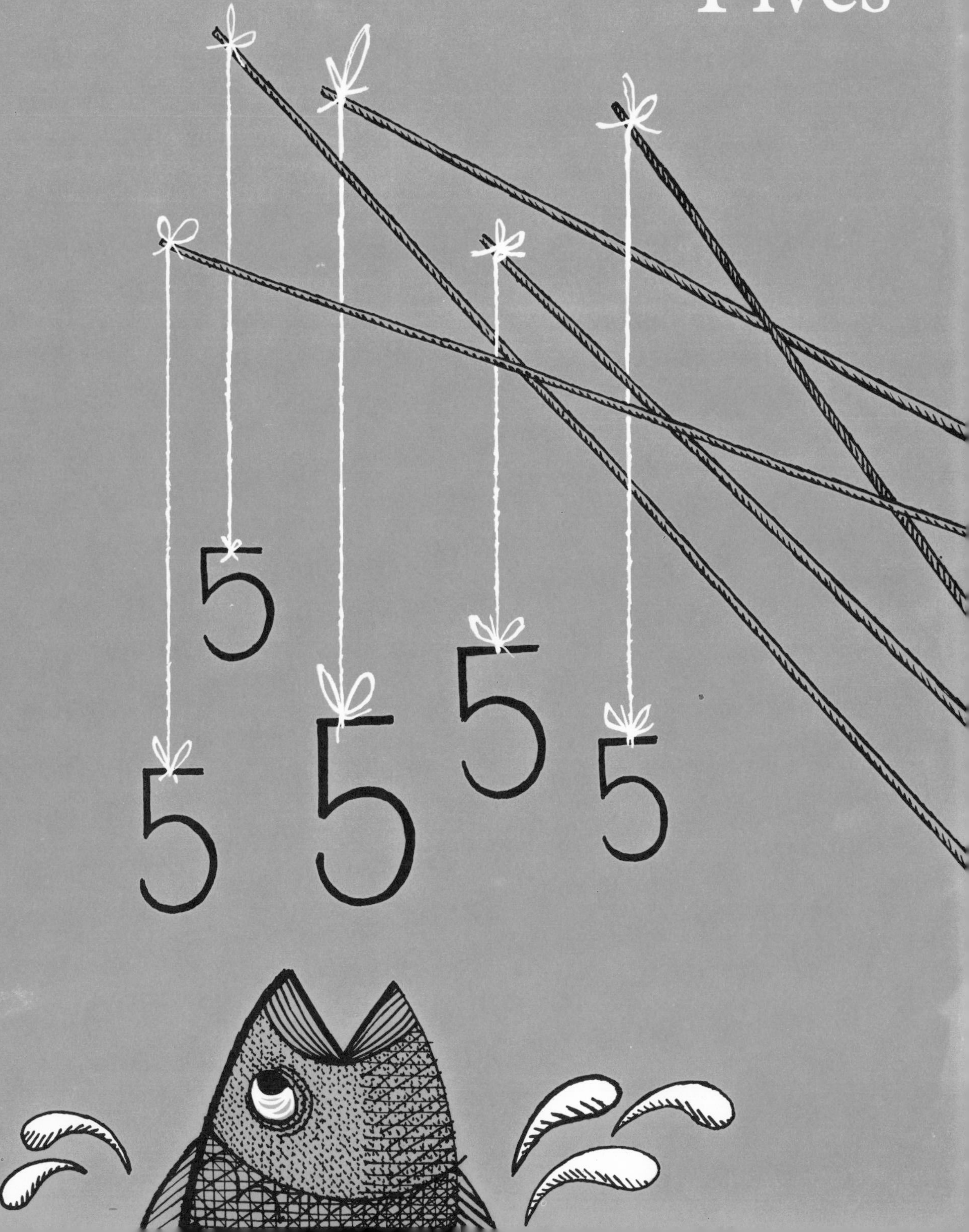

# Contents

# Five

Five little children,
Hand in hand,
Went to dig
The yellow sand.

Five little castles,
Trim and neat,
Soon were standing
At their feet.

Five little starfish
Standing near,
Said, "Five little houses!—
Let's live here!"

CLARE TRINGRESS

# With a Hop, and a Skip, and a Jump

With a hop, and a skip, and a jump—
ONE, TWO,
Stand up straight like the soldiers do.

With a hop, and a skip, and a jump—
THREE, FOUR,
Crouch down small, very near to the floor.

With a hop, and a skip, and a jump—
FIVE, SIX,
Rock from side to side like a clock that ticks.

With a hop, and a skip, and a jump—
SEVEN, EIGHT,
Pretend that your feet are a very heavy weight.

With a hop, and a skip, and a jump—
NINE, TEN,
Creep along slowly, like a lion to his den.

W. O'NEILL

# Six Little Mice

Six little mice sat down to spin,
Pussy passed by, and she peeped in.
"What are you at, my little men?"
"Making coats for gentlemen."
"Shall I come in and bite off your threads?"
"No, no, Miss Pussy, you'll snip off our
      heads."
"Oh, no, I'll not, I'll help you to spin."
"That may be so, but you don't come in!"

TRADITIONAL

# Ten Little Squirrels

Ten little squirrels sat on a tree,
The first two said, "Why, what do we see?"
The next two said, "A man with a gun,"
The next two said, "Let's run, let's run,"
The next two said, "Let's hide in the shade,"
The next two said, "Why, we're not afraid!"
But, "Bang!" went the gun, and away they
      all run.

TRADITIONAL

# Black Monkeys

One black monkey swinging on a tree.
Two black monkeys paddling in the sea.

Three black monkeys playing on a swing.
Four black monkeys dancing in a ring.

Five black monkeys drinking lemonade.
Six black monkeys digging with a spade.

Seven black monkeys wearing sailor hats.
Eight black monkeys waving cricket bats.

Nine black monkeys standing on their heads.
Ten black monkeys sleeping in their beds.

RUTH AINSWORTH

# A Counting Rhyme

One little,
Two little,
Three little pigs,
Small and fat and pink,
Fell into a tub of tar
And turned as black as ink.
Four little,
Five little,
Six little pigs
Went to see the moon;
They found it colder than they thought,
And came back very soon.
Seven little,
Eight little,
Nine little pigs
Went to look for gold;
They found it in a pickle-jar,
At least, that's what I'm told.

M. M. STEPHENSON

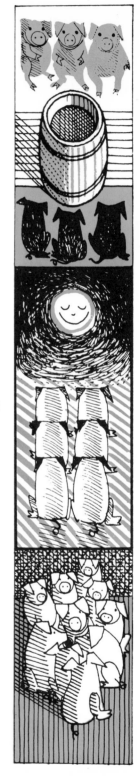

9

# One, Two

One, two,
What shall I do?

Three, four
Play on the floor.

Five, six,
Build with bricks.

Seven, eight,
Make a gate.

Nine, ten,
Knock it down again.

RUTH AINSWORTH

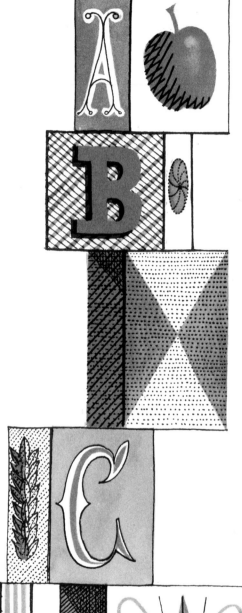

# Greedy Tom

Jimmy the Mowdy
Made a great crowdy;
Barney O'Neal
Found all the meal;
Old Jack Rutter
Sent two stone of butter;
The Laird of the Hot
Boiled it in his pot;
And Big Tom of the Hall
He supped it all.

UNKNOWN

# Ten Little Dicky-birds

One little dicky-bird,
Hopped on my shoe;
Along came another one,
And that made two.

*Chorus*   Fly to the tree-tops;
Fly to the ground;
Fly, little dicky-birds,
Round and round.

Two little dicky-birds,
Singing in a tree;
Along came another one,
And that made three.

*Chorus*

Three little dicky-birds,
Came to my door;
Along came another one,
And that made four.

*Chorus*

Four little dicky-birds
Perched on a hive;
Along came another one,
And that made five.
            *Chorus*

Five little dicky-birds
Nesting in the ricks;
Along came another one,
And that made six.
            *Chorus*

Six little dicky-birds
Flying up to heaven;
Along came another one,
And that made seven.
            *Chorus*

Seven little dicky-birds
Sat upon a gate;
Along came another one,
And that made eight.
            *Chorus*

Eight little dicky-birds
Swinging on a line;
Along came another one,
And that made nine.

> *Chorus*

Nine little dicky-birds
Looking at a hen;
Along came another one,
And that made ten.

> *Chorus*

A. W. I. BALDWIN

# Acorn Bill

I made a little acorn man
And inked his smiling face,
I stuck four pins for legs and arms,
Each firmly in its place.

I found a tiny acorn cup
To put upon his head,
And then I showed him to my friends;
"Meet Acorn Bill," I said.

RUTH AINSWORTH

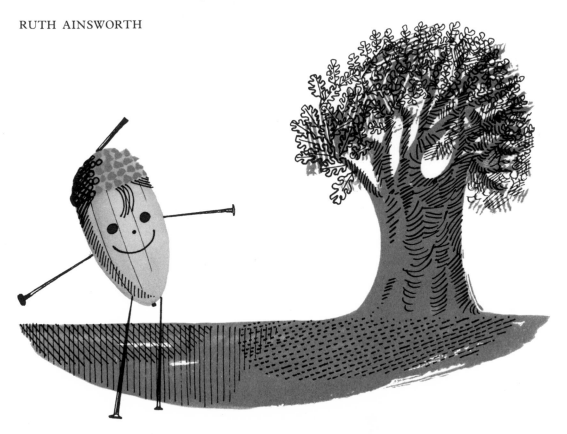

# Fun with my Shadow

My shadow walks the way I walk
And runs the way I run,
And if I hop along the road
He hops behind for fun.

I told him just this evening
Before I came to bed,
I thought I'd rather like it
If he went in front instead.

He said,
"Well that's peculiar—
I've often thought it too,—
I've got a big tremendous urge
To show YOU what to do!"

I wonder what he'll show me.
I hope his tricks are new;
I'll learn them really quickly
And show them all to you!

CLARE TRINGRESS

2

# Who Likes the Rain?

"I," said the duck. "I call it fun,
For I have my pretty red rubbers on;
They make a little three-toed track
In the soft, cool mud—quack! quack!"

"I," cried the dandelion, "I,
My roots are thirsty, my buds are dry,"
And she lifted a tousled yellow head
Out of her green and grassy bed.

Sang the brook: "I welcome every drop,
Come down, dear raindrops; never stop
Until a broad river you make of me,
And then I will carry you to the sea."

"I," shouted Ted, "for I can run,
With my high-top boots and raincoat on,
Through every puddle and runlet and pool
I find on the road to school."

UNKNOWN

# There Lived a Little Man

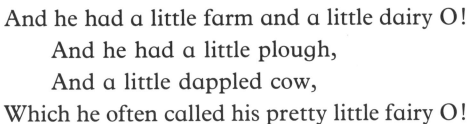

Once there lived a little man
Where a little river ran,
And he had a little farm and a little dairy O!
And he had a little plough,
And a little dappled cow,
Which he often called his pretty little fairy O!

And his dog he called Fidèle,
For he loved his master well,
And he had a little pony for his pleasure O!
In a sty, not very big,
He'd a frisky little pig
Which he often called his little piggy
treasure O!

TRADITIONAL

# Ride Away

Ride away, ride away,
Johnny shall ride,
And he shall have pussy-cat
Tied to one side.
He shall have little dog
Tied to the other,
And Johnny shall ride
To see his grandmother.

NURSERY RHYME

# Following the Music

I stamp my feet
  And wriggle my toes
And clap my hands
  As the music goes.

I reach to the sky
  And touch the ground.
Up and down to the
  Music sound.

I rock to and fro
  The way the wind blows;
It's fun to go
  Where the music goes.

HILDA I. ROSTRON

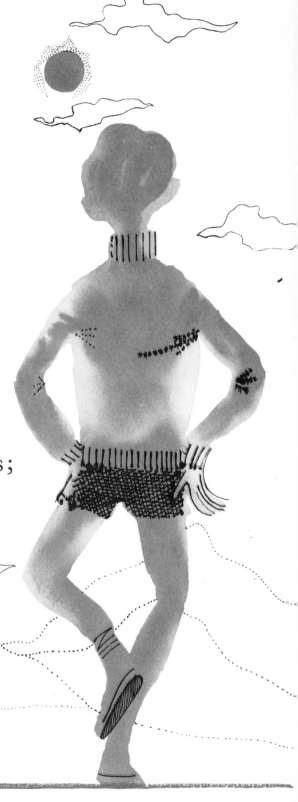

# Higglety, Pigglety, Pop

Higglety, pigglety, pop!
The dog has eaten the mop;
The pig's in a hurry,
The cat's in a flurry,
Higglety, pigglety, pop!

UNKNOWN

# You Do It Too

I can jump, jump, jump
Like a kangaroo,
With a bump, bump, bump.
Can you do it too?

I can creep along
Like a jungle cat.
My steps are long,
Are yours like that?

I can spread my wings
Like a bird in the sky,
And fly round in rings—
Would you like to try?

MARGARET LANGFORD

23

# The Dove's Song

Coo-pe-coo, coo-pe-coo,
    Me and my poor two,
Two sticks across, and a little bit of moss,
    And it will do, do, do.

UNKNOWN

# Dogs

I had a little dog,
    and my dog was very small.
He licked me in the face,
    and he answered to my call.
Of all the treasures that were mine,
    I loved him best of all.

FRANCES CORNFORD

# The Snowman

We look out of the window
To see the snowman stand
Cold and white
All day and night,
With an icicle in his hand.

The snowman looks in the window
To see us having our tea;
The fire burns red
As we eat our bread
And he thinks, "How HOT they must be!"

RUTH AINSWORTH

26

# Clocks and Watches

Our great
Steeple clock
Goes TICK – TOCK,
TICK – TOCK;

Our small
Mantel clock
Goes TICK–TACK, TICK–TACK,
TICK–TACK, TICK– TACK;

Our little
Pocket watch
Goes Tick-a-tacker, tick-a-tacker,
Tick-a-tacker, tick.

UNKNOWN

# Pitty Patty Polt

Pitty Patty Polt!
Shoe the wild colt,
    Here a nail,
    There a nail,
Pitty Patty Polt!

UNKNOWN

# Catkin

I have a little pussy,
    And her coat is silver grey;
She lives in a great wide meadow
    And she never runs away.
She always is a pussy,
    She'll never be a cat
Because—she's a pussy willow!
    Now what do you think of that!

UNKNOWN

# Birds in the Garden

Greedy little sparrow,
    Great big crow,
Saucy little tom-tits
    All in a row.

Are you very hungry,
    No place to go?
Come and eat my breadcrumbs,
    In the snow.

UNKNOWN

# After a Bath

After my bath
I try, try, try
to wipe myself
till I'm dry, dry, dry.

Hands to wipe
and fingers and toes
and two wet legs
and a shiny nose.

Just think how much
less time I'd take
if I were a dog
and could shake, shake, shake.

AILEEN FISHER

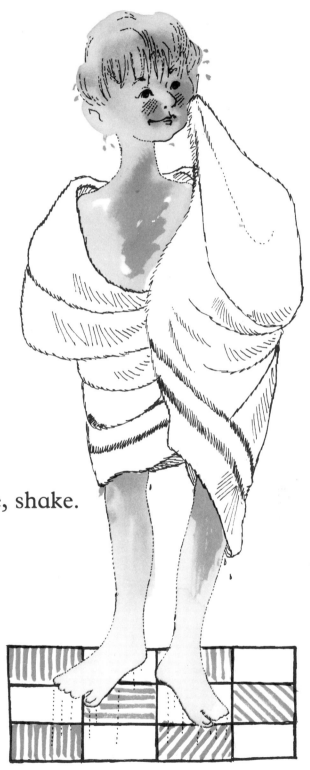

# You, North Must Go

You, North must go,
To a hut of snow;
You, South in a trice,
To an island of spice;
You, off to China,
And sit on a hill!
And you to that chair,
And be five minutes still!

UNKNOWN

# Runaway Engine

Run away engine,
Ricketty Rack,
Running around the
Railway track.

All the way there and
All the way back,
Run away engine
Ricketty Rack.

MOLLIE CLARKE

3

# A Boy Went Walking

One day a boy went walking,
And walked into a store.
He bought a pound of sausage meat,
And laid it on the floor.

The boy began to whistle—
He whistled up a tune,
And all the little sausages
Danced around the room.

UNKNOWN

# As I Went up the Garden

As I went up the garden
I found a little farthing;
I gave it to my mother,
To buy a little brother;
My brother was a sailor,
He sailed across the sea,
And all the fish that he could catch
Were one, two, three.

TRADITIONAL

# Dame Trot and her Cat

Dame Trot and her cat
Sat down for to chat;
The Dame sat on this side,
And Puss sat on that.

"Puss," says the Dame,
"Can you catch a rat,
Or a mouse in the dark?"
"Purr," says the cat.

TRADITIONAL

# Monday

Every Monday
(The day after Sunday)
It's splish day and splosh day,
With all the clothes to wash day,
I hope it will keep fine.

Usually
By Tuesday
They've dried it all
And iron'd it all
Pillowcases, sheets and shirts
And handkerchiefs (some mine).

But I love wash day
Steamy, soapy splosh day
With all the clothes a-billowing,
And flying on the line.

UNKNOWN

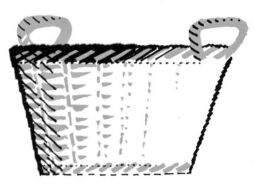

# Sing-song

Bread and milk for breakfast,
    And woollen frocks to wear,
And a crumb for robin redbreast
    On the cold days of the year.

CHRISTINA ROSSETTI

# Riddles

What thing am I?

I have legs,
One, two, three, four,
But I cannot walk
Across the floor.
      *Answer :*   A CHAIR

I have teeth,
Long and white,
They are sharp
But I cannot bite.
      *Answer :*   A COMB

I can prick your finger
And make you cry,
But I can't see a thing
With my one little eye.

Answer : A NEEDLE

RUTH AINSWORTH

# Riddles

I am round like a ball
And I live in the sky,
You will see me at night
If you look up high.

Answer : THE MOON

You can see me in the country,
You can see me in the town.
Sometimes I am up,
And sometimes I am down.
If the sun shines very brightly
I am never there at all;
But everyone can see me
When the rain begins to fall.

Answer : UMBRELLA

I can walk on this
If it's wet or dry;
I can put it in a pail
And make a pie.
If I hold it in my hands
It will trickle through,
I can find it at the seaside—
And so can you.

                *Answer :*   SAND

UNKNOWN

# The Mouse

Hush!
     Come
         Quietly,
I've just seen a mouse!
I'm not quite sure,
But I think he's in the house.

He may be in the pantry,
Looking for his tea;
He may be in a tiny hole,
Peeping out at me.

He isn't very handsome,
He isn't very fat.
His tail is long and straggly,
And wriggles—just like that!

So please tread softly,
And tiptoe by the wall;
For if he hears you coming
      He won't
            be there
                  at all!

M. M. STEPHENSON

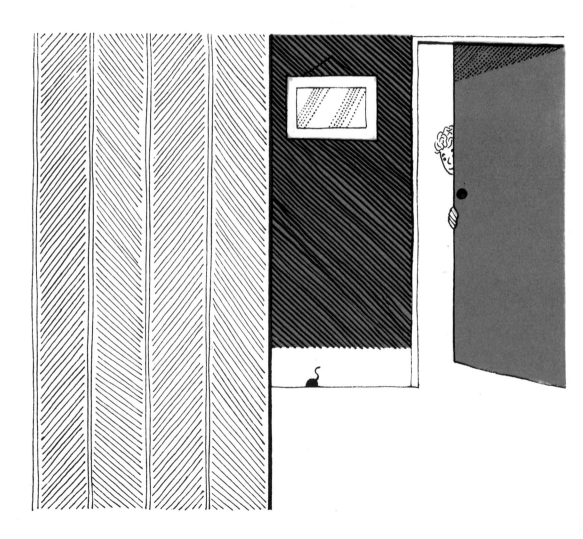

# Jump—Jump—Jump

Jump—jump—jump—
    Jump away
From this town into
    The next, today.

Jump—jump—jump—
    Jump over the moon;
Jump all the morning,
    And all the noon.

Jump—jump—jump—
    Jump all night;
Won't our mothers
    Be in a fright?

Jump—jump—jump—
    Over the sea;
What wonderful wonders
    We shall see.

Jump—jump—jump—
    Jump far away;
And all come home
    Some other day.

KATE GREENAWAY

# Kindness to Animals

Riddle cum diddle cum dido,
My little dog's name is Fido;
    I bought him a wagon,
    And hitched up a dragon,
And off we both went for a ride, oh!

Riddle cum diddle cum doodle,
My little cat's name is Toodle;
    I curled up her hair,
    But she only said, "There!
You have made me look just like a poodle!"

Riddle cum diddle cum dinky,
My little pig's name is Winkie;
    I keep him quite clean
    With the washing machine,
And I rinse him all off in the sinkie.

LAURA RICHARDS

# Cats

Cats sleep
Anywhere,
Any table,
Any chair,
Top of piano,
Window-ledge,
In the middle,
On the edge,
Open drawer,
Empty shoe,
Anybody's
Lap will do,
Fitted in a
Cardboard box,
In the cupboard
With your frocks—
Anywhere!
They don't care!
Cats sleep
Anywhere.

ELEANOR FARJEON

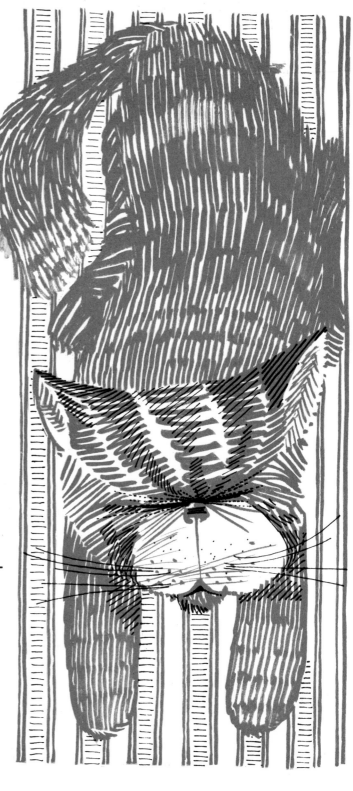

# Timothy Dan

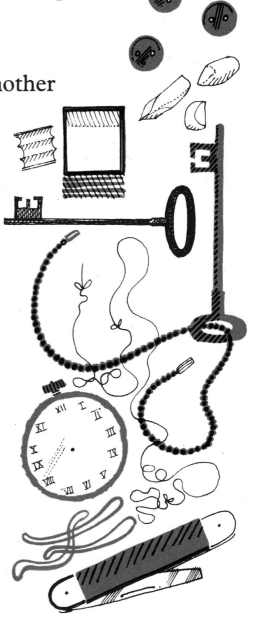

Timothy Dan
Is a very rich man,
And he keeps all his wealth in his pocket:
Four buttons, a box,
The keys of two clocks,
And the chain of his grandmother
      Margaret's locket;
A big piece of string
(It's a most useful thing),
A watch without hands,
And three rubber bands,
Five glassy marbles,
Some tail-ends of chalk,
A squeaker that once
Made a golliwog talk,
A broken-down penknife
With only one blade,
And a little toy boat
That his grandfather made.

You'd never believe
(Hearing such a long list)

That there's room in each pocket
For one little fist;
You'd never believe
That the smallest of boys
Could carry so much
In his wee corduroys.

JOHN D. SHERIDAN

Sixes

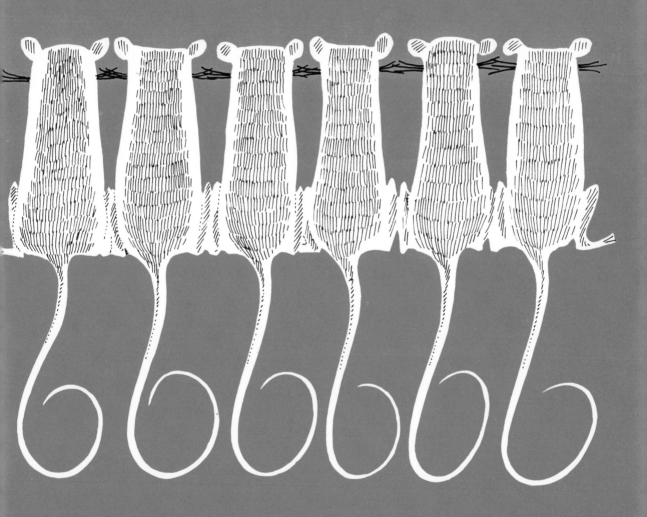

# Contents

# Pockets

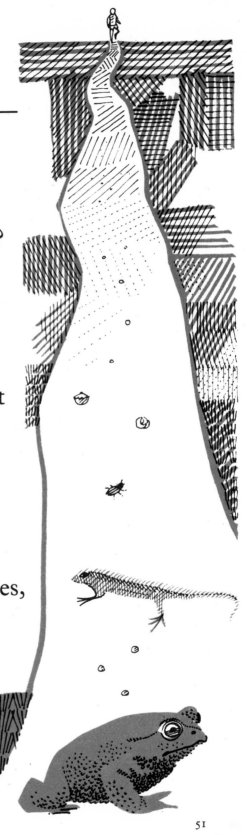

A child should have pockets—
Supposing on the road
He runs across a beetle,
Or a lizard, or a toad?
However will he carry them?
Whatever will he do
If he hasn't got a pocket
To put them into?

A child should have a pocket
On which he fairly dotes!
Not one or two, but many
In his little waistcoats—
And one will be for money
He finds on the road,
And one for cakes and cookies,
And one for hoptoads!

SUSAN ADGER WILLIAMS

# Zoo Manners

Be careful what
    You say or do
When you visit the animals
    At the Zoo.

Don't make fun
    Of the Camel's hump—
He's very proud
    Of his noble bump.

Don't laugh too much
    At the Chimpanzee—
He thinks he's as wise
    As you or me.

And the Penguins
    Strutting round the lake
Can understand
    Remarks you make.

Treat them as well
          As they do you,
And you'll always be welcome
          At the Zoo.

EILEEN MATHIAS

## The Holiday

Five little goblins went to town,
Their caps were red and their jackets brown,
They'd sixpence each—that was
          half-a-crown!
So five little goblins went to town.

One bought a lollipop, large and round,
One bought some caramels—half a pound,
One bought a whistle that wouldn't make a
          sound;
One lost his sixpence and it couldn't be found.

The last bought a puppy with eyes of brown.
Its tail curled up and its ears hung down,
The fourth found his sixpence and soon lost
    his frown,
When five little goblins came from town.

M. STREDDER

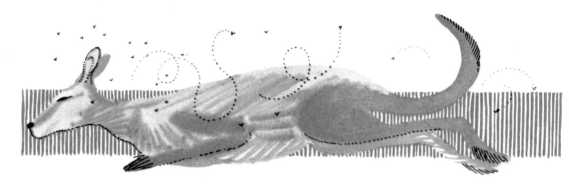

## The Kangaroo

Old Jumpety-Bumpety-Hop-and-Go-One
Was lying asleep on his side in the sun.
This old Kangaroo, he was whisking the flies
(With his long glossy tail) from his ears and
    his eyes.
Jumpety-Bumpety-Hop-and-Go-One
Was lying asleep on his side in the sun,
Jumpety-Bumpety-Hop!

UNKNOWN

# On the Ning Nang Nong

On the Ning Nang Nong
Where the cows go Bong!
And the monkeys all say Boo!
There's a Nong Nang Ning
Where the trees go Ping!
And the tea pots Jibber Jabber Joo.
On the Nong Ning Nang
All the mice go Clang!
And you just can't catch 'em when they do!
So it's Ning Nang Nong!
Cows go Bong!
Nong Nang Ning!
Trees go Ping!
Nong Ning Nang!
The mice go Clang!
What a noisy place to belong,
Is the Ning Nang Ning Nang Nong!

SPIKE MILLIGAN

# The Dustman

Every Thursday morning
Before we're quite awake,
Without the slightest warning
The house begins to shake
  With a Biff! Bang!
  Biff! Bang! Biff!
It's the Dustman, who begins
  (Bang! Crash!)
To empty all the bins
Of their rubbish and their ash
  With a Biff! Bang!
  Biff! Bang! Bash!

CLIVE SANSOM

# November Glow

November is a cold month,
Freezing, foggy, grey,
But I have found some things that glow
To chase the grey away.

The pillar-box is shining red,
Red mail-vans stand close by;
The fire's flames glow red and gold,
Laughing as they leap high.

Red berries in the hedges
For hungry birds to eat;
Red buses splashing through the rain
Along the busy street.

November is a cold month,
As everybody knows;
I wear a bright red woolly scarf,
And Robin's red breast glows!

HILDA I. ROSTRON

# The Sandcastle

I built a castle in the sand—
The finest castle in the land,
And from the turret, standing high,
My flag waved proudly in the sky:
And then I built a wall around
To help to keep it safe and sound.
I had a drawbridge made of wood,
And round the moat my soldiers stood.
But since I built it yesterday,
The sea has washed it all away.
I'll build my next one on the beach
Beside the deck-chairs—out of reach!

M. M. STEPHENSON

# The Curliest Thing

The squirrel is the curliest thing
        I think I ever saw;
He curls his back, he curls his tail,
        He curls each little paw,
He curls his little vest so white,
        His little coat so grey—

He is the most curled-up wee soul
    Out in the woods at play!

UNKNOWN

# I Caught a Fish

I caught a little fish one day—
    A baby fish, I think.
It made me jump, I heard it say,
    "I want another drink."
I didn't know a fish could speak—
    That's why I jumped, you see.
It spoke in just a tiny squeak,
    Not loud like you and me.
"You want a drink? You greedy fish,
    "You've had enough, I know.
"I'll put you on my Mummy's dish
    "With salt to make you grow."
"You'd better not," replied the fish,
    "My Dad's a great big whale,
"And if you put me on a dish
    "He'll kill you with his tail."
I'm not afraid of whales, I'm not;

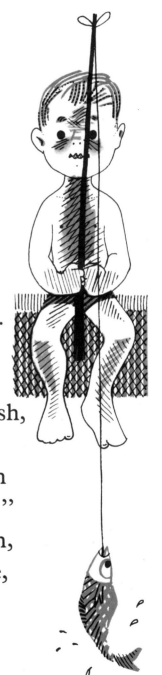

I'd eat one for my tea,
But I was angry with the tot,
So threw it in the sea.
The little fish was full of joy,
It gave its head a nod.
"Good-bye," it squeaked, "you silly boy,
"My Daddy's just a cod."

BERTRAM MURRAY

## Some Fishy Nonsense

Timothy Tiggs and Tomothy Toggs,
They both went a-fishing for pollothywogs;
They both went a-fishing
Because they were wishing
To see how the creatures would turn into
frogs.

Timothy Tiggs and Tomothy Toggs,
They both got stuck in the bogothybogs;
They caught a small minnow,
And said 'twas a sin oh!
That things with no legs should pretend to
be frogs.

LAURA RICHARDS

# Toadstools

It's not a bit windy,
It's not a bit wet,
The sky is as sunny
As summer, and yet
Little umbrellas are
Everywhere spread,
Pink ones, and brown ones,
And orange, and red.

I can't see the folks
Who are hidden below;
I've peeped, and I've peeped
Round the edges, but no!
They hold their umbrellas
So tight and so close
That nothing shows under,
Not even a nose.

ELIZABETH FLEMING

# There are Big Waves

There are big waves and little waves,
    Green waves and blue,
Waves you can jump over,
    Waves you dive thro',
Waves that rise up
    Like a great water wall,
Waves that swell softly
    And don't break at all,
Waves that can whisper,
    Waves that can roar,
And tiny waves that run at you
    Running on the shore.

ELEANOR FARJEON

# Down the Stream the Swans all Glide

Down the stream the swans all glide;
It's quite the cheapest way to ride.
Their legs get wet,
Their tummies wetter:
I think after all
The bus is better.

SPIKE MILLIGAN

# Three Mice

Three little mice walked into town,
Their coats were grey, and their eyes were
      brown.

Three little mice went down the street,
With woolwork slippers upon their feet.

Three little mice sat down to dine
On curranty bread and gooseberry wine.

Three little mice ate on and on,
Till every crumb of the bread was gone.

Three little mice, when the feast was done,
Crept home quietly one by one.

Three little mice went straight to bed,
And dreamt of crumbly, curranty bread.

CHARLOTTE DRUITT COLE

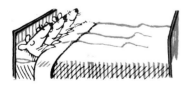

# Tails

A tail is such a useful thing,
The monkey uses his to swing.
The kangaroo can strike a blow
While standing on his tail, you know.

When pussy's tail waves in the air
It means she's angry—so beware!
But when my puppy plays with me
He wags his little tail with glee!

If only I'd a tail to swish
I'd swim as smoothly as a fish.
Or if a monkey's tail were mine
I'd swing from Mummy's washing line.

But I go swimming in the pool,
And I can climb the ropes at school . . .
And I eat cakes and strawberry jam,
So maybe I'll stay as I am!

IVY RUSSELL

# The Rainbow Fairies

Two little clouds one summer's day
    Went flying through the sky.
They went so fast they bumped their heads,
    And both began to cry.

Old Father Sun looked out and said:
    "Oh, never mind, my dears,
I'll send my little fairy folk
    To dry your falling tears."

One fairy came in violet,
    And one in indigo,
In blue, green, yellow, orange, red—
    They made a pretty row.

They wiped the cloud tears all away,
    And then, from out the sky,
Upon a line the sunbeams made
    They hung their gowns to dry.

L. M. HADLEY

5

# Autumn's Passing

Bonfire smoke swirls upward
    Golden leaves fall down,
Nuts and berries show themselves
    Red and shining brown.

Swallows now have left us,
    Flown across the seas;
Squirrels are so busy
    Storing nuts in trees.

Hedgehog is bed-making,
    Ready for his sleep;
Robin, gay and curious,
    Stops to take a peep.

Listen to the rustle
    Where crisp leaves are found
Strewn in many colours,
    Carpeting the ground.

Who, then, can be passing,
    This bright wind-swept day?
Surely it is Autumn
    Going on her way.

HILDA I. ROSTRON

# Red-currant Jelly

Red-currant jelly,
And black-currant jam,
And an apple for tea—
How lucky I am!
But I'd rather have honey
Than black-currant jam.

"Will you give me honey
You little brown bee?"
"Yes, I'll give you honey,
If you will give me
The jelly and jam
That was meant for your tea."

"A sweet rosy apple
And honey for me,
And jelly and jam
For the little brown bee."

The little brown bee sings
"How happy I am;
I have red-currant jelly
And black-currant jam."

M. M. STEPHENSON

# Hide and Seek

When I am alone, and quite alone,
I play a game, and it's all my own.

I hide myself
Behind myself,
And then I try
To find myself.

I hide in the closet,
Where no one can see;
Then I start looking
Around for me.

I hide myself
And look for myself;
There once was a shadow
I took for myself.

I hide in a corner;
I hide in the bed;
And when I come near me
I pull in my head!

A. B. SHIFFRIN

# Rufty and Tufty

Rufty and Tufty were two little elves
    Who lived in a hollow oak tree.
They did all the cooking and cleaning
      themselves
    And often asked friends in to tea.

Rufty wore blue, and Tufty wore red,
    And each had a hat with a feather.
Their best Sunday shoes they kept under the
      bed—
    They were made of magic green leather.

Rufty was clever and kept the accounts,
    But Tufty preferred to do cooking.
He could make a fine cake without weighing
      amounts—
    And eat it when no one was looking!

ISABELL HEMPSEED

# Run a Little

Run a little this way,
    Run a little that!
Fine new feathers
    For a fine new hat.
A fine new hat
    For a lady fair—
Run around and turn about
    And jump in the air.

Run a little this way,
    Run a little that!
White silk ribbon
    For a black silk cat.
A black silk cat
    For the Lord Mayor's wife—
Run around and turn about
    And fly for your life!

JAMES REEVES

# Waiting

Waiting, waiting, waiting
    For the party to begin;
Waiting, waiting, waiting
    For the laughter and din;
Waiting, waiting, waiting
    With hair just so
And clothes trim and tidy
    From top-knot to toe.
The floor is all shiny,
    The lights are ablaze;
There are sweetmeats in plenty
    And cakes beyond praise.
Oh the games and dancing,
    The tricks and the toys,
The music and the madness
    The colour and noise!
Waiting, waiting, waiting
    For the first knock on the door—
Was ever such waiting,
    Such waiting before?

JAMES REEVES

# Cottage

When I live in a Cottage
I shall keep in my Cottage

Two different Dogs,
Three creamy Cows,
Four giddy Goats,
Five Pewter Pots,
Six silver Spoons,
Seven busy Beehives,
Eight ancient Appletrees,
Nine red Rosebushes,
Ten teeming Teapots,
Eleven chirping Chickens,
Twelve cosy Cats with their kittenish
        Kittens and
One blessed Baby in a Basket.

That's what I'll have when I live in my
        Cottage.

ELEANOR FARJEON

# The Cat

The black cat yawns,
Opens her jaws,
Stretches her legs,
And shows her claws.

Then she gets up
And stands on four
Long stiff legs
And yawns some more.

She shows her sharp teeth,
She stretches her lip,
Her slice of a tongue
Turns up at the tip.

Lifting herself
On her delicate toes,
She arches her back
As high as it goes.

She lets herself down
With particular care,
And pads away
With her tail in the air.

MARY BRITTON MILLER

# Sleepy John

"I'm much too tired,"
Said Sleepy John,
"To put my shoes and stockings on.
In fact, this dressing's
Just a bore,
I think I'll go to sleep once more!"
He went to sleep,
And dreamed,—
(Did John,)
His stockings would not
Be put on;
His shoes ran races on their own,
And oh! how all his clothes had grown!
He wakened up
And jumped out quick,
And dressed himself
In half a tick.
"When next I go to sleep,"
Said John,
"I'll keep my shoes and stockings
ON!"

CLARE TRINGRESS

# Grandad's Pipe

After tea, while others knit,
Two children, tired, excited, sit
On Grandad's knee as the pipe is lit.
    "I'm lighter-up!" said she.
    "I'm blower-out!" said he.

She strikes the match. When sparks are
        growing,
He blows it out with one great blowing,
And Grandad sucks till the pipe is glowing.
    "I'm lighter-up!" said she.
    "I'm blower-out!" said he.

The smoke climbs up in clouds of blue
To melt or pierce the ceiling through,
And all their troubles vanish too.
    "I'm lighter-up!" said she.
    "I'm blower-out!" said he.

IAN SERRAILLIER

75

# The Cupboard

I know a little cupboard,
    With a teeny tiny key,
And there's a jar of Lollypops
    For me, me, me.

It has a little shelf, my dear,
    As dark as dark can be,
And there's a dish of Banbury Cakes
    For me, me, me.

I have a small fat grandmamma,
    With a very slippery knee,
And she's Keeper of the Cupboard,
    With the key, key, key.

And when I'm very good, my dear,
    As good as good can be,
There're Banbury Cakes, and Lollypops
    For me, me, me.

WALTER DE LA MARE

# Choosing Shoes

New shoes, new shoes,
Red and pink and blue shoes,
Tell me, what would you choose,
    If they'd let us buy?

Buckle-shoes, bow shoes,
Pretty pointy-toe shoes,
Strappy, cappy low shoes;
    Let's have some to try.

Bright shoes, white shoes,
Dandy-dance-by-night shoes—
Perhaps-a-little-tight shoes,
    Like some? so would I.

BUT

Flat shoes, fat shoes,
Stump-along-like-that-shoes,
Wipe-them-on-the-mat-shoes,
    That's the sort they'll buy.

FFRIDA WOLFE

77

# The Chickens

Said the first little chicken
 With a queer little squirm,
"I wish I could find
 A fat little worm."

Said the next little chicken
 With an odd little shrug,
"I wish I could find
 A fat little slug."

Said the third little chicken
 With a sharp little squeal,
"I wish I could find
 Some nice yellow meal."

Said the fourth little chicken
 With a small sigh of grief,
"I wish I could find
 A little green leaf."

Said the fifth little chicken
     With a faint little moan,
"I wish I could find
     A wee gravel stone."

"Now, see here," said the mother,
     From the green garden patch,
"If you want any breakfast,
     Just come here and scratch."

UNKNOWN

## Cock a Doodle Doodle Doo

Cock a doodle doodle do,
     Cock a doodle dandy!
I have got a pretty maid,
     And she is very handy.
She washes all her knives and forks,
     And platters in the sea, Sir;
She scrubs the floor with cabbage stalks,
     As clean as clean can be, Sir.

Cock a doodle doodle do,
    Cock a doodle didy!
I have got a pretty maid,
    And she is very tidy.
She sweeps the cobwebs off the sky,
    And rubs with all her might, Sir,
The sun, and moon, and stars so high,
    Or how could they look bright, Sir?

UNKNOWN

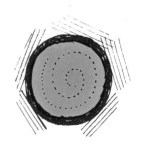

## There was a Little Dog

There was a little dog sitting by the fireside,
Out popped a little coal,
And in the little doggie's tail
It burnt a little hole.
Away ran the little dog, to seek a little pool
To cool his little tail,
And for want of a better place,
He popped it in the pail,
He popped it in the pail,
And wiggle, waggle, wiggle, waggle,
    wiggle, waggle, wiggle, waggle,
Went the doggie's tail.

UNKNOWN

Sevens

# Contents

# The Elephant

Here comes the elephant
Swaying along
With his cargo of children
All singing a song:
To the tinkle of laughter
He goes on his way,
And his cargo of children
Have crowned him with may.
His legs are in leather
And padded his toes:
He can root up an oak
With a whisk of his nose:
With a wave of his trunk
And a turn of his chin
He can pull down a house,
Or pick up a pin.

Beneath his grey forehead
A little eye peers;
Of what is he thinking
Between those wide ears?
Of what does he think?

If he wished to tease,
He could twirl his keeper
Over the trees:
If he were not kind,
He could play cup and ball
With Robert and Helen,
And Uncle Paul:
But that grey forehead,
Those crinkled ears,
Have learned to be kind
In a hundred years:
And so with the children
He goes on his way
To the tinkle of laughter
And crowned with the may.

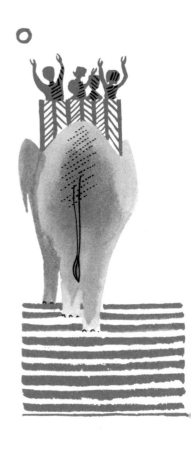

HERBERT ASQUITH

## The Magic Window

Our window is a magic frame
With pictures never twice the same.
Sometimes it frames a sunset sky,
Where clouds of gold and purple lie.
And sometimes, on a windless night,
It holds a great moon round and white.

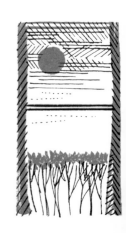

Sometimes it frames a lawn and flowers,
Where children play through summer hours.
Sometimes, a tree of gold and red
And grass where crisp brown leaves are shed.
And sometimes it shows wind-blown rain
Or snowflakes against the pane.
Our window frames all lovely things
That every changing season brings.

ELEANOR HAMMOND

# Cows

Half the time they munched the grass,
And all the time they lay
Down in the water-meadows, the lazy month
of May,
A-chewing,
A-mooing,
To pass the hours away.

"Nice weather," said the brown cow.
"Ah," said the white.
"Grass is very tasty."
"Grass is all right."

Half the time they munched the grass,
And all the time they lay
Down in the water-meadows, the lazy month
of May,
A-chewing,
A-mooing,
To pass the hours away.

"Rain coming," said the brown cow.
"Ah," said the white.
"Flies is very tiresome."
"Flies bite."

Half the time they munched the grass,
And all the time they lay
Down in the water-meadows, the lazy month
of May,
A-chewing,
A-mooing,
To pass the hours away.

"Time to go," said the brown cow.
"Ah," said the white.
"Nice chat," "Very pleasant."
"Night." "Night."

Half the time they munched the grass,
And all the time they lay
Down in the water-meadows, the lazy month
of May,
A-chewing,
A-mooing,
To pass the hours away.

JAMES REEVES

## There Once Was a Puffin

Oh, there once was a Puffin
Just the shape of a muffin,
And he lived on an island
In the
        bright
                blue
                        sea.

He ate little fishes,
That were most delicious,
And he had them for supper
And he
                    had
                                them
                                            for tea.

But this poor little Puffin,
He couldn't play nothin',
For he hadn't anybody
To
            play
                        with
                                    at all.

So he sat on his island,
And he cried for a while, and
He felt very lonely,
And he
            felt
                        very ..
                                    small.

Then along came the fishes,
And they said, "If you wishes,
You can have us for playmates,
Instead
      of
          for
              tea."

So they now play together,
In all sorts of weather,
And the puffin eats pancakes,
Like you
      and
          like
              me.

FLORENCE PAGE JAQUES

## Jack Frost

    Look out! look out!
    Jack Frost is about!
He's after our fingers and toes;
    And, all through the night,
    The gay little sprite
Is working where nobody knows.

He'll climb each tree,
So nimble is he,
His silvery powder he'll shake;
To windows he'll creep,
And while we're asleep,
Such wonderful pictures he'll make.

Across the grass,
He'll merrily pass,
And change all its greenness to white;
Then home he will go,
And laugh, "Ho! ho! ho!
What fun I have had in the night!"

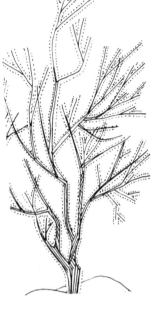

CECILY E. PIKE

## The Farmyard

Up was I on my father's farm
On a May day morning early,
Feeding of my father's cows
On a May day morning early.
With a moo, moo here, and a moo, moo there,
Here a moo, there a moo, here a pretty moo;
Six pretty maids come and gang along o' me
To the merry green fields and the farmyard.

> Can you make up some more animal verses?

Up was I on my father's farm
On a May day morning early,
Feeding of my father's goats
On a May day morning early.
With a nan, nan here, and a nan, nan there,
Here a nan, there a nan, here a pretty nan;
Six pretty maids come and gang along o' me
To the merry green fields and the farmyard.

UNKNOWN

# The Tub

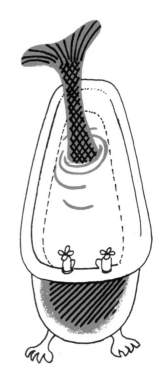

My tub is an aquarium
In which the fish is me;
I like to think that I am some
Strange monster of the sea.

Sometimes a mighty whale I am,
The monarch of the deep,
And other times I am a clam
And almost fall asleep!

Then I become a sinking ship
That signals her distress
And tells of a disastrous trip
By yelling "S O S!"

And then I am a lifeboat, manned
By gallant lads and true,
I save myself from drowning and
I get a medal, too!

And then I hear my mother's shout,
That calls me back to shore,
And GEE! I have to clamber out
And be a boy once more! !

GEORGE S. CHAPPELL

# Under-the-Table Manners

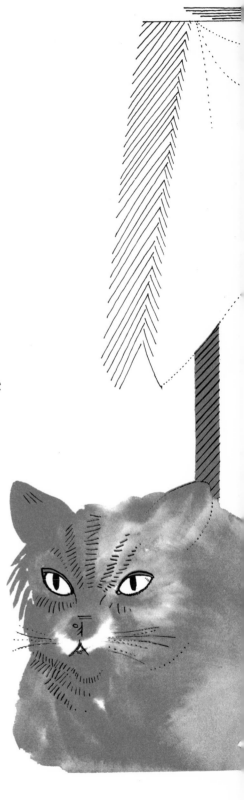

It's very hard to be polite
    If you're a cat.
When other folks are up at table
Eating all that they are able,
    You are down upon the mat
    If you're a cat.

You're expected just to sit
    If you're a cat.
Not to let them know you're there
By scratching at the chair,
    Or a light, respected pat
    If you're a cat.

You are not to make a fuss
    If you're a cat.
Tho' there's fish upon the plate
You're expected just to wait,
    Wait politely on the mat
    If you're a cat.

UNKNOWN

# Red in Autumn

Tipperty-Toes, the smallest elf,
Sat on a mushroom by himself,
Playing a little tinkling tune
Under the big round harvest moon;
And this is the song that Tipperty made
To sing to the little tune he played.

"Red are the hips, red are the haws,
Red and gold are the leaves that fall,
Red are the poppies in the corn,
Red berries on the rowan tall;
Red is the big round harvest moon,
And red are my new little dancing shoon."

ELIZABETH GOULD

# Dame Duck's Lecture

Close by the margin of the brook,
The old duck made her nest,
Of straw and leaves and withered grass,
And down from her own breast.

And there she sat for four long weeks,
Through rainy days and fine,
Until the ducklings all came out,
Four, five, six, seven, eight, nine.

One peeped out from beneath her wing,
One scrambled on her back.
"That's very rude," said old Dame Duck,
"Get off—quack, quack, quack, quack."

"Too close," said Dame Duck, shoving out
The egg-shells with her bill.
Besides, it never suits young ducks
To keep them sitting still.

So, rising from her nest, she said,
"Now, children, look at me.
A well-bred duck should waddle
From side to side—d'ye see?"

"Yes," said the little ones, and then
She went on to explain:
"A well-bred duck turns in its toes,
And do try again."

"Yes," said the ducklings, waddling on.
"That's better," said the mother,
"But well-bred ducks walk in a row
Straight, one behind the other."

"Yes," said the little ducks again,
All waddling in a row;
"Now to the pond," said old Dame Duck.
Splash, splash, and in they go.

UNKNOWN

## Animals' Houses

Of animals' houses
    Two sorts are found—
Those which are square ones
    And those which are round.

Square is a hen-house,
    A kennel, a sty:
Cows have square houses
    And so have I.

A snail's shell is curly,
    A bird's nest round;
Rabbits have twisty burrows
    Underground.

But the fish in the bowl
    And the fish at sea—
Their houses are round
    As a house can be.

JAMES REEVES

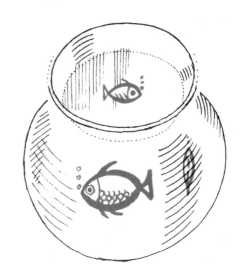

# The Dormouse

A raindrop fell down on a dormouse's nose,
And the wind whistled, "Whoo!" at his
        ears and his toes.
"Brrr!" cried the dormouse, and shivered
        with cold,
"The rain is too wet
And the wind is too bold."

7

Where is the dormouse?
He's lying asleep,
Curled in a tight little drowsy heap;
Safe from the snow, and the wind,
        and the rain,
He'll dream in his nest till the spring
        comes again.

M. M. STEPHENSON

# My Dog

Have you seen a little dog anywhere about?
A raggy dog, a shaggy dog, who's always
        looking out
For some fresh mischief which he thinks he
        really ought to do.
He's very likely, at this minute, biting
        someone's shoe.

If you see that little dog, his tail up in the air,
A whirly tail, a curly tail, a dog who doesn't
        care
For any other dog he meets, not even for
        himself;
Then hide your mats, and put your meat
        upon the topmost shelf.

If you see a little dog, barking at the cars,
A raggy dog, a shaggy dog, with eyes like
        twinkling stars,
Just let me know, for though he's bad, as
        bad as bad can be;
I wouldn't change that dog for all the
        treasures of the sea!

EMILY LEWIS

## Caravans

I've seen caravans
Going to the fair!
    Come along,
    Come along,
Let's go there!

Hurrah! roundabouts,
Lovely little swings,
    Coconuts,
    Coconuts,
Heaps of things!

See all the animals
Waiting for the show;
    Elephants,
    Elephants,
Let's all go!

Look! There's a tiger
Watching baby bears;
    Come away,
    Come away,
How he stares!

Hark! how the music plays
Ready for the fun!
    Come along,
    Come along,
Let's all run.

IRENE THOMPSON

# Rabbit and Lark

"Under the ground
    It's rumbly and dark
And interesting,"
    Said Rabbit to Lark.

Said Lark to Rabbit,
    "Up in the sky
There's plenty of room
    And it's airy and high."

"Under the ground
    It's warm and dry.
Won't you live with me?"
    Was Rabbit's reply.

"The air's so sunny.
    I wish you'd agree,"
Said the little Lark,
    "To live with me."

But under the ground
    And up in the sky,
Larks can't burrow
    Nor rabbits fly.

So Skylark over
    And Rabbit under
They had to settle
    To live asunder.

And often these two friends
    Meet with a will
For a chat together
    On top of the hill.

JAMES REEVES

## Autumn Woods

I like the woods
    In autumn
When dry leaves hide the ground,
When the trees are bare
And the wind sweeps by
With a lonesome rushing sound.

I can rustle the leaves
    In autumn
And I can make a bed
In the thick dry leaves
That have fallen
From the bare trees
Overhead.

JAMES S. TIPPETT

## I Like

I like to stay at home and put
The kettle on the fire;
I like to watch the yellow flames
So suddenly leap higher!
I like to hear the kettle sing
Before the steam comes out.
But best of all, I like to pour
    The water from its spout!

I like to make the toast for tea
And hold it to the fire,
And snatch it back just as the flames
So suddenly leap higher!
I like to make the edges crisp
And crinkly like a shell.
But best of all, I like to spread
     The butter really *well*!

But mother fills the kettle up
And puts it on the fire
Because, she says, the yellow flames
So suddenly leap higher!

She makes the toast, and crinkles it,
And spreads the butter thick—
The grown-ups always have the fun—
     I'll grow up—pretty quick!

CLARE TRINGRESS

# The Road to China

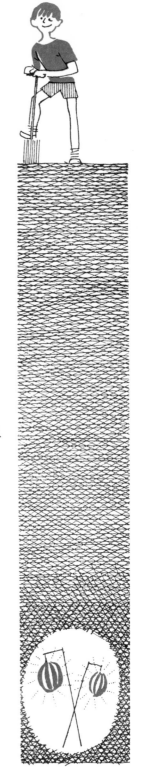

I learned today the world is round
    Like my big rubber ball,
With China on the other side,
    Down there below us all.

And so I went and dug a hole,—
    I started it at eight,—
And dug and dug and dug and dug,
    Beside the garden gate.

And oh, I thought, what fun 't will be
    To get a ladder tall,
And climb right down to China through
    The hole behind the wall!

What fun to walk through little streets
    All lit with lanterns queer!
Each man will have a pigtail, and
    How strange the talk I'll hear!

To think the road to China lies
    Just by our garden wall!
Then Daddy came and said, "Ho! Ho!
    That's not the way at all!

"To get to China, you must sail
    For days across the sea!"
Why there's no short cut through the earth
    Seems very queer to me!

And still I sit beside my hole
    And dream and dream away,
Of that strange, far-off country where
    They've night time in our day!

OLIVE BEAUPRÉ MILLER

## As I Looked Out

As I looked out on Sunday last,
A fat little pig went hurrying past.
Over his shoulders he wore a shawl,
Although it didn't seem cold at all.
I waved at him, but he didn't see me,
For he never so much as looked at me.
Once again, when the moon was high,
I saw the little pig hurrying by;
Back he came at a terrible pace,
The moonlight shone on his little pink face,
And he smiled with a smile that was quite
        content.
But never I knew where that little pig went.

UNKNOWN

# Chairoplane Chant

If every one had a flying machine
The size of a small armchair,
Then day after day, in the promptest way
I'd go out to take the air.
I'd shift a lever and press a brake,
And buzz into the blue.
Oho, the bushels of air I'd take,
Flying to call on you!

As I skirted a steeple and skimmed a roof,
With engine whirring loud,
I'd meet you coming for dear life, humming
Around the rim of a cloud.
We'd dodge a swallow and duck a crow,
And you would cry, "Whoopee,
I was going to call on you, you know—
Were you coming to call on me?"

It's rather awkward to chat, of course,
From a high-geared chairoplane,
So we'd buzz away. But the very next day
We'd meet in a sky-blue lane,
With wind in our wings, and the way all
        clear,
And I'd sing, "Ho, halloo,
Were you coming to call on me? O dear,
I was going to call on you!"

NANCY BYRD TURNER

# The Owl and the Pussy-cat

The Owl and the Pussy-cat went to sea
        In a beautiful pea-green boat,
They took some honey, and plenty of money,
        Wrapped up in a five-pound note.
The Owl looked up to the stars above,
        And sang to a small guitar,
"O lovely Pussy! O Pussy, my love,
        What a beautiful Pussy you are,
                You are,
                You are,
        What a beautiful Pussy you are!"

Pussy said to the Owl, "You elegant fowl!
    How charmingly sweet you sing!
O let us be married! too long we have tarried:
    But what shall we do for a ring?"
They sailed away for a year and a day,
    To the land where the Bong-tree grows,
And there in a wood a Piggy-wig stood,
    With a ring at the end of his nose,
            His nose,
            His nose,
    With a ring at the end of his nose.

"Dear Pig, are you willing to sell for one
        shilling,
    Your ring?" Said the Piggy, "I will."
So they took it away, and were married next
        day
    By the Turkey who lived on the hill.

They dined upon mince, and slices of quince,
    Which they ate with a runcible spoon;
And hand in hand, on the edge of the sand,
    They danced by the light of the moon,
        The moon,
        The moon,
    They danced by the light of the moon.

EDWARD LEAR

## Some One

Some one came knocking
    At my wee, small door;
Some one came knocking,
    I'm sure—sure—sure;
I listened, I opened,
    I looked to left and right,
But nought there was a-stirring
    In the still dark night;

Only the busy beetle
    Tap-tapping in the wall,
Only from the forest
    The screech owl's call,
Only the cricket whistling
    While the dewdrops fall,
So I know not who came knocking,
    At all, at all, at all.

WALTER DE LA MARE

## Grasshopper Green

Grasshopper Green is a comical chap;
    He lives on the best of fare.
Bright little trousers, jacket, and cap,
    These are his summer wear.

Out in the meadow he loves to go,
    Playing away in the sun;
It's hopperty, skipperty, high and low,
    Summer's the time for fun.

Grasshopper Green has a quaint little house;
　　It's under the hedge so gay,
Grandmother Spider, as still as a mouse,
　　Watches him over the way.

Gladly he's calling the children, I know,
　　Out in the beautiful sun;
It's hopperty, skipperty, high and low,
　　Summer's the time for fun.

UNKNOWN

## Who Stole the Nest?

"To-whit! to-whit! to-whee!
Will you listen to me?
Who stole four eggs I laid,
And the nice nest I made?"

"Not I," said the cow, "moo-oo!
Such a thing I'd never do.
I gave you a wisp of hay,
But did not take your nest away;
Not I," said the cow, "moo-oo!
Such a thing I'd never do."

"Bob-o-link! Bob-o-link!
Now, what do you think?
Who stole a nest away
From the plum-tree today?"

"Not I," said the dog, "bow-wow!
I wouldn't be so mean, I vow.
I gave some hairs the nest to make,
But the nest I did not take;
Not I," said the dog, "Bow-wow!
I wouldn't be so mean, I vow."

"Coo-'oo! coo-'oo! coo-'oo!
Let me speak a word or two:
Who stole that pretty nest
From little Robin Redbreast?"

"Not I," said the sheep; "oh, no!
I wouldn't treat a poor bird so;
I gave the wool the nest to line,
But the nest was none of mine.
Baa! baa!" said the sheep; "oh, no!
I wouldn't treat a poor bird so."

"Caw! caw!" cried the crow,
"I should like to know
What thief took away
A bird's nest today."

"Chuck! chuck!" said the hen,
"Don't ask me again;
Why, I haven't a chick
Would do such a trick."

"We all gave her a feather,
And she wove them together.
I'd scorn to intrude
On her and her brood.
Chuck! chuck!" said the hen,
"Don't ask me again."

"Chirr-a-whirr! chirr-a-whirr!
We will make a great stir.
Let us find out his name,
And all cry—For shame!"

UNKNOWN

# The Land of the Bumbley Boo

In the land of the Bumbley Boo
The people are red, white and blue,
They never blow noses,
Or ever wear closes,
What a sensible thing to do!

In the Land of the Bumbley Boo
You can buy Lemon pie at the Zoo;
They give away Foxes
In little Pink Boxes
And Bottles of Dandelion Stew.

In the Land of the Bumbley Boo
You never see a Gnu,
But thousands of Cats
Wearing trousers and hats
Made of Pumpkins and Pelican Glue!

*Chorus*
Oh, the Bumbley Boo! the Bumbley Boo!
That's the place for me and you!
So hurry! Let's run!

The train leaves at one!
For the Land of the Bumbley Boo!
The wonderful Bumbley Boo-Boo-Boo!
The Wonderful Bumbley BOO ! ! !

SPIKE MILLIGAN

## The Sun's Frolic

"Now," said the Sun, when winter had gone,
"I'll have some fun with everyone.
I'll wake all the sleepyheads,
Snoring and dreaming;
(How little they dream
Of my planning and scheming),
I'll breathe on their noses
Their tailsies and toesies,
YOU SEE IF I DON'T—"
AND HE DID!

He went to the dormouse
Asleep in his nest,
And he shone and he shone
Till he sank in the west.
The next day he shone
On the squirrels and trees,

And the next day on hedges
And beetles and bees.

"I like all this hurry and scurry," he said,
"I'll make them all scramble and get out of
      bed,
YOU SEE IF I DON'T—"
AND HE DID!

CLARE TRINGRESS

## The Boy with the Little Bare Toes

He ran all down the meadow, that he did,
    The boy with the little bare toes.
The flowers they smelt so sweet, so sweet,
And the grass it felt so funny and wet
And the birds sang just like this—"chereep!"
    And the willow-trees stood in rows.
      "Ho! ho!"
    Laughed the boy with the little bare toes.

Now the trees had no insides—how funny!
　　　Laughed the boy with the little bare toes,
And he put in his hand to find some money
Or honey—yes, that would be best—oh, best!
But what do you think he found, found, found?
Why, six little eggs all round, round, round,
And a mother-bird on the nest,
　　　　　　Oh, yes!
　　The mother-bird on her nest.

He laughed, "Ha! ha!" and he laughed,
　　　"He! he!"
　　The boy with the little bare toes.
But the little mother-bird got up from her
　　　place
And flew right into his face, ho! ho!
And pecked him on the nose, "Oh, oh!"
　　　Yes, pecked him right on the nose.
　　　　　"Boo! Boo!"
　　Cried the boy with the little bare toes.

F. W. HARVEY

# A Prayer for Little Things

Please God, take care of little things,
The fledglings that have not their wings,
Till they are big enough to fly
And stretch their wings across the sky.

And please take care of little seeds,
So small among the forest weeds,
Till they have grown as tall as trees
With leafy boughs, take care of these.

And please take care of drops of rain
Like beads upon a broken chain,
Till in some river in the sun
The many silver drops are one.

Take care of small new lambs that bleat,
Small foals that totter on their feet,
And all small creatures ever known
Till they are strong to stand alone.

And please take care of children who
Kneel down at night to pray to You,
Oh please keep safe the little prayer
That like the big ones asks Your care.

ELEANOR FARJEON

## Familiar Friends

The horses, the pigs,
And the chickens,
The turkeys, the ducks,
And the sheep!
I can see all my friends
From my window
As soon as I waken
From sleep.

The cat on the fence
Is out walking.
The geese have gone down
For a swim.
The pony comes trotting
Right up to the gate;
He knows I have candy
For him.

The cows in the pasture
Are switching
Their tails to keep off
The flies.
And the old mother dog
Has come out in the yard
With five pups to give me
A surprise.

JAMES S. TIPPETT

## The Cobbler

Wandering up and down one day,
I peeped into a window over the way;
And putting his needle through and through,
There sat a cobbler making a shoe:
For the world he cares never the whisk of a
        broom—
All he wants is elbow-room.
    Rap-a-tap, tick-a-tack-too,
    That is the way he makes a shoe!

Over laths of wood his bits of leather
He stretches and fits, then sews together;
He puts his wax ends through and through;

And still as he stitches, his body goes too:
For the world he cares never the whisk of a
    broom—
      Rap-a-tap-tap, tick-a-tack-too,
      This is the way he makes a shoe!

With his little sharp awl he makes a hole
Right through the upper and through the
    sole;
He puts in one peg, and he puts in two,
And chuckles and laughs as he hammers
    them through:
For the world he cares never the whisk of a
    broom—
All he wants is elbow-room.
      Rap-a-tap-tap, tick-a-tack-too,
      This is the way to make a shoe!

UNKNOWN

## Chicks and Ducks

"The time is drawing very near,"
    Said Mrs Hen one day,
"For all my little chickens dear
    To break their shells away.

How proud and joyful I shall be
    When through the yard I go
With all my little family
    Behind me in a row."
Crack go the eggs beneath her wings,
    Four little heads peep out,
And soon four fluffy little things
    Are running all about.
She leads them proudly through the yard,
    And gains the field beyond;
"For here," she thinks, "They're safe from
        harm."—
    When they espy a pond.
As fast as little legs can go
    They all start off. "Come back,
Come back, my dears," she cries in woe;
    They only answer, "Quack!"
"Alas! alas! they'll all be drowned;
    They're in the pond," she clucks;
But, lo! they're swimming safe and sound,
    For they were all four ducks!

UNKNOWN

# A Road Might Lead to Anywhere

"A road might lead to anywhere—
 To harbour towns and quays,
Or to a witch's pointed house
 Hidden by bristly trees.
It might lead past the tailor's door,
 Where he sews with needle and thread,
Or by Miss Pim the milliner's,
 With her hats for every head.
It might be a road to a great, dark cave
 With treasure and gold piled high,
Or a road with a mountain tied to its end,
 Blue-humped against the sky.
Oh, a road might lead you anywhere—
 To Mexico or Maine.
But then, it might just fool you, and—
 Lead you back home again!"

UNKNOWN

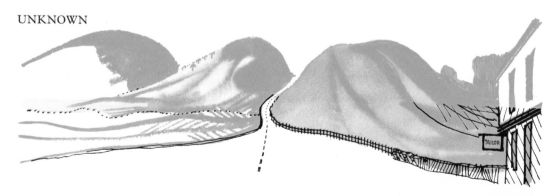

# The Leaves

The leaves had a wonderful frolic,
    They danced to the wind's loud song,
They whirled, and they floated, and
       scampered,
    They circled and flew along.

The moon saw the little leaves dancing,
    Each looked like a small brown bird.
The man in the moon smiled and listened,
    And this is the song he heard.

The North Wind is calling, is calling,
    And we must whirl round and round,
And then when our dancing is ended
    We'll make a warm quilt for the ground.

UNKNOWN

# Donkey Riding

Were you ever in Quebec,
Stowing timbers on a deck,
Where there's a king in his golden crown
    Riding on a donkey?

Hey ho, and away we go,
    Donkey riding, donkey riding,
Hey ho, and away we go,
    Riding on a donkey.

Were you ever in Cardiff Bay,
Where the folks all shout, Hooray!
Here comes John with his three months' pay,
    Riding on a donkey?

Hey ho, and away we go,
    Donkey riding, donkey riding,
Hey ho, and away we go,
    Riding on a donkey.

Were you ever off Cape Horn,
Where it's always fine and warm?
See the lion and the unicorn
    Riding on a donkey.

Hey ho, and away we go,
    Donkey riding, donkey riding,
Hey ho, and away we go,
    Riding on a donkey.

UNKNOWN